T0115194

An Educator's Guide to Program Planning and Service Delivery

PHYLLIS M. WILSON, Ph.D.

authorHOUSE®

AuthorHouse™
1663 Liberty Drive
Bloomington, IN 47403
www.authorhouse.com
Phone: 833-262-8899

Published by AuthorHouse 04/08/2021

ISBN: 978-1-6655-2127-7 (sc)
ISBN: 978-1-6655-2126-0 (e)

Library of Congress Control Number: 2021906336

Print information available on the last page.

Introduction

Over forty years of my life was spent working as an educator. I began my career as a teacher in the Chicago Public Schools. It ended after serving eleven years as the superintendent of a school district in Illinois. During my years, I held many positions and was responsible for the educational services of thousands of children. When I served as the Assistant Superintendent for Curriculum and Instruction in a 64,000 student school district, it became extremely clear to me, that the professional development provided to administrators and teachers was critical to the progress and success of students. As a teacher, I had been a participant in workshops and inservices. As an administrator, I was now given the responsibility for determining and planning the workshops for everyone. A big shift that now required careful thought and careful selection of what works best and for whom. My intensity and need to do my best and do my job well caused me to acquire many skills in the professional development arena. These acquired skills are what I wish to share with you today in the hope that it will lighten your load and create a high performing, highly skilled environment for the students you serve. May this book help you meet every goal that you have set for your staff.

Acknowledgements

I wish to thank the many people who contributed to the successes in my career. You walked the long journey with me and experienced both the good times and the bad times. I will be forever grateful that you were a part of my life.

Dr. Rosa Smith-My role model

Charyll Colstock, Aracelis Popadich, Sandra Zalewski-You took every dream, every idea, and every vision I had and made them a reality.

Carol Sossong-You were my right and left hands when it came to implementing curricular initiatives and programs.

Anna White, Brenda Byrnes, Brenda Gorman, Julie Rice Zurek-You exemplified all that a Principal should be and made your schools the star locations that they were. Martini Girls Forever!

Danielle Gustafson-You are still there for me whenever I have a tech problem.

Deb Ziech, Jeff Pritz-You supported me as board members throughout my tenure. I always knew I could count on you.

All of the administrators, principals,teachers, custodial staff, paraprofessionals, clerical staff, curriculum specialists-You were a part of my family and helped to make the district a great place to work.

Mica Wilson-You are the best Daughter anyone could ever have. You shared me with thousands of students while continuing to carve your own path in life.

In Memoriam

Helen C. Fairchild-You never stopped being proud of me and taking care of my daughter on the many days that job responsibilities had to be a priority. My career never faltered because you never failed me.

Gerald Bersano-You loved the district and the students. You gave your all to make sure that everyone was well served.

UIC

Student Engagement

Student Engagement Examples

Two approaches to student engagement include:

The Genius Club-Students need to be encouraged and repeatedly reminded of the great capacity they have for learning. The Genius Club identifies all students involved operating at the level of genius and high performance. The club has both a symbol and a pledge that is repeated each time the club is in session.

*Children for Peace-In order to teach the emotional capacity for empathy and kindness to others, the Children for Peace initiative was formulated as a districtwide effort. Each day students, in every school, recited the Peace Pledge as a way of reinforcing courtesy and acts of kindness to everyone in the school environment. Students contributed financially to various causes whether the amount given was a penny or a nickel (My free and reduced lunch numbers were 67%). The concept behind the act of giving was to teach my students that they needed to not only receive benefits; but, also give back to others.

The Children for Peace model included art activities that followed a specific theme, musical band and song performances, all culminating in a spring time performance at our local theater. Parents and community members were invited to attend the performance and view the student art on display in the theater lobby. The theater administrator was a partner with the district and allowed us to charge 3-5 dollars for tickets. The theater, newly renovated and beautifully designed and showcased our students in an amazing way.

This initiative received statewide recognition and an award from the B'Hai religious organization.

- *Much gratitude goes to Principal Anna White for leading this initiative; and, to John Armstrong, the Band Director, teachers, administrators, school staff, and all of the parents who supported our program.

Children For Peace Project

September 2002

Developed by:
Dr. Phyllis M. Wilson
Mrs. Carol Sossong
Mrs. Sandra Zalewski
Ms. Anna White

Table of Contents

Purpose

The Purpose of the "Children For Peace" project is to raise the consciousness of children about utilizing peaceful strategies and methods to interact with others in the school setting, the neighborhood setting, and the community at large.

Definition

The "Children For Peace" project will require students to pledge to resolve conflicts and disagreements in peaceful ways. Students will resolve to perform one peaceful act a day (i.e. Not engaging in an argument but choosing silence or walking away) in the school setting. Students will also be asked to perform one act of kindness a day in their neighborhood and community.

The intention of a raised scrutiny on peaceful acts is to assist students to create an atmosphere conducive to cooperation and caring. Students will utilize hands-on-engaged learning techniques and technology to view the world stage as a setting for peace. Through the analysis of the actions occurring around them, students will be able to analyze circumstances and actions of others to identify peaceful options and alternatives that could be applied.

Children for Peace

Peace Pledge

I am a Peace Builder,
I pledge to praise people,
to give up put downs.
I will build peace at home, at school,
and in my community every day.

Genius Club Summary

Students need to believe in themselves and feel confident that they can accomplish the tasks set before them. Many students who attend do not have that level of self confidence resulting in lowered self- esteem and an inclination to fail in the school setting. The Genius club is designed to instill in students a higher level of confidence and belief in the competence level that will result in improved performance in the school setting. The Genius club is designed to be an after school tutoring and mentoring program guaranteed to increase the academic achievement levels of those participating in the program.

The Genius Club program will provide tutors trained in the best way to help students learn. One tutor will be provided for every 10 students attending the program. It is the specific methods being used and the small number of students being tutored in each group that adds to student success. All students will be taught the Genius Pledge and begin each session by reciting the pledge. The pledge serves to remind students that they are now in the genius category and that is how each student should see himself or herself as a genius capable of conquering their circumstances and their environment and any task placed before them. Any child entering the program will feel like a genius when the program ends. A genius who will be able to follow specific steps in every learning situation and for every subject. A mentor will also be assigned to remain in contact and follow up on student's continuing progress after the program ends. This program can make it happen.

The genius Club

Genius Club Pledge

I am a genius. I can accomplish every goal I set for myself. I am determined to be a high achiever.

I will work hard. I will have a plan for my life. I will be all that I can be. This, I promise.

Staff Engagement

Staff Engagement Examples

The presentations of " It's in Your hands" and "Creating a Culture of Caring" were designed to remind teachers and other staff members of the significant role that they played in the education of district students.

The "Ritz of Education" was a summary of the kinds of behaviors and public interactions expected of all staff. A list of expected behaviors was given to each employee to be used to model the kinds of actions that represented the district in the best way possible.

Star Employees-Staff members who modeled the expected behaviors and conduct were selected and recognize with a star statue.

Improved Performance Schools- Schools that showed significant continuous improvement would be recognized at the staff opening of the year event. Along with the star statue, the schools would receive a financial award as well.

There Are Only Phenomenal Teachers In District 86

Phenomenal teachers:

- ✓ Accept the fact that many aspects of their students lives are outside of their control
- ✓ Realize that during the school day they have numerous opportunities to plant positive messages and foster seeds of resiliency in their students.
- ✓ Make choices every day to offer their students both academic and personal tools for success.
- ✓ Have high expectations and assist students in rising to the level of those expectations.

Gail L. Thompson, Through Ebony Eyes: What Teachers Need to Know But Are Afraid to Ask About African American Students, p.131.

What Does A Great School Look Like?

1. It is a place where staff members collaborate with others. We need partners to help us do our work.
2. It is a place with an "almost stoic determination to do whatever needs to be done to make the school great" (p.20 Good to Great).
3. It is a place "infected with an incurable need to produce results" (p.30 Good to Great).
4. It is a place where the right people are on the bus.
5. It is a place where obstacles are viewed as challenges to overcome. No excuses are made.

From "Good to Great" by Todd Whitaker

"What Great Teachers Do Differently"

1. Great teachers never forget that it is people, not programs that determine the quality of a school.
2. Great teachers establish clear expectations at the start of the year and follow them consistently as the year progresses.
3. When a student misbehaves, great teachers have on goal: to keep that behavior from happening again.
4. Great teachers have high expectations for students but even higher expectations for themselves.
5. Great teachers know who is the variable in the classroom: They are. Good teachers consistently strive to improve, and they focus on something they can control – their own performance.

- Fourteen Things That Matter Most by Todd Whitaker

Who Are We?

Joliet Public Schools District 86 considers itself the center for educational excellence for the 10,174 students enrolled in grades Pre-Kindergarten through Eighth. The District covers 26.4 square miles and the majority of Joliet, Illinois. The District has approximately 1,300 employees, including 600 teachers.

Who Do We Serve?

The District is most proud of the diversity represented by our student population.

The population consists of:

44% Hispanic
33% African-American
19% Caucasian; and
4% Other

The District provides instruction for all children in the curricular areas of language arts, mathematics, science, social science, fine arts, physical development and health. In addition Early Childhood Education is provided for 318 students; English Language Learner services for 893 students; Special Education for 1,170 students; and Full Day Kindergarten for 1004 students.

There are:

12 Elementary Schools
4 Junior High Schools
4 Magnet Schools
1 Early Childhood Center
1 Gifted Center
1 Alternative School

The District wide free and reduced price lunch percentage is 72%.

What Is Our Purpose?

The District exists for the sole reason of providing high quality education for **all** students in the cleanest and safest buildings possible, without excuses.

The Ritz of Education Joliet District 86

Joliet District 86 is a place where the genuine care and comfort
of our learning community is our highest mission.
We pledge to provide the finest education
and facilities for our community
in a warm, relaxed learning environment.

- Our motto is "We Ladies and Gentlemen Serving Ladies and Gentlemen of all ages." As educational professionals, we must treat all our students, guests, and each other with respect and dignity.

- A foundation of exceptional service to all stakeholders can be provided by following three simple steps of service:

1) Make everyone feel welcome and comfortable.
2) Anticipate a person's needs and be compliant with those needs.
3) Communicate with a positive attitude at all times.

- Never lose the opportunity to resolve a problem. Whoever receives a complaint will own it and help resolve it.

- Be an ambassador of your school in and outside of the workplace. Always speak positively. Communicate any concern to the appropriate person.

- Think safety first. Each employee is responsible for creating a safe, secure, and accident-free environment for everyone. Be aware of all fire and safety emergency procedures and report any security risks immediately.

Table of Contents

EXHIBIT A

District Goals

Revised July 2006

Elementary Level

GOAL I: All students will read at or above grade level by third grade as measured by Thinklink Learning Predictive Assessment.

GOAL II: All students will meet or exceed state math standards as measured by ISAT.

Junior High Level

GOAL I: All students will read at or above grade level by seventh grade as measured by Thinklink Learning Predictive Assessment.

GOAL II: All students will be prepared for high school English and ninth grade Algebra I placement by eighth grade as measured by Thinklink Learning Predictive Assessment.

GOAL Ill: All students will meet or exceed state math standards as measured by ISAT.

100% of District 86 students will graduate from high school as measured by school district surveys to receiving high schools.

80% of District 86 students will graduate from postsecondary schools as measured by surveys sent to former students.

EXHIBIT B

Name:____________________

School:____________________

Principal Planning Form Checklist

		DATE DUE	YES	NO
1.	Partners in Learning Agreement has been given to parents (**Exhibit Q/R**)	2nd week of school	______	______
2.	Parent Communication forms have been developed	9/26/08	______	______
3.	School Discipline brochure has been developed	8/29/08	______	______
4.	Student Goal Setting Occurs	Ongoing throughout year	______	______
5.	Building Evaluation Form has been implemented (**Exhibit C**)	End of each semester	______	______
6.	Planning Focus process has been implemented (**Exhibit D/E**)	10/1/08	______	______

7.	Student articulation occurs	Ongoing throughout year	______	______
8.	School rules are posted	1st week of school	______	______
9.	School language is posted (**Exhibit F**)	1st week of school	______	______
10.	Discipline Expectations (**Exhibit J**)	1st week of school	______	______
11.	Best practices are utilized	Ongoing throughout year	______	______
12.	The Ritz Carlton Model for customer service has been implemented (**Exhibit G**)	1st day staff returns	______	______
13.	Ritz Checklist (**Exhibit H**)	9/26/08	______	______
14.	Direction Questions have been completed (**Exhibit I**)	9/26/08	______	______
15.	Principal Self Evaluation Form has been completed (**Exhibit K**)	9/26/08	______	______
16.	Principal Focus Activities have been used to determine building strategies (**Exhibit L**)	Ongoing throughout year	______	______

17.	Principal Evaluation Form	9/26/08		
18.	Principal's Action Plan	9/26/08		
19.	Assistant Principal Academic Advisor Evaluation Form	3/3/09		

EXHIBIT C

Building Evaluation Form

Attitude	A	B	C	D
Effort	A	B	C	D
Professional Knowledge	A	B	C	D
Student Results	A	B	C	D
Student/Teacher Interaction	A	B	C	D
Teacher/Parent Interaction	A	B	C	D
Parental Involvement/Communication	A	B	C	D
Zero-based Suspensions/Expulsions	A	B	C	D

This form should be completed at the end of each semester with all staff giving input into grade selection. Small groups can be used with an average of all small group scores serving as the final score. Any area identified as below C should have improvement strategies developed and implemented. **Please return completed form quarterly (September/December/March/May) to Dr. Wilson.**

EXHIBIT D

Elementary Planning Focus

1. Language Rich Class Implementation
2. Refinement of discipline model
3. Selection/Implementation of best practices to improve student performance

    a) In cooperation with BLT, select a specific ‘ target goal for ISAT improvement
    b) Specific activities to ensure that all students reading by 3rd grade.

3. Continued implementation of district initiatives
4. Display of school and classroom posters that emphasize work to be accomplished and district priorities as well as grade level academic expectations
5. School-wide improvement focus area - select one area that will be top priority in building
6. Applying Ritz Carlton model to customer service
7. Making District Learning Agreement meaningful and doing necessary follow up actions with parents

EXHIBIT E

Junior High Planning Focus

1. Increased use of data analysis to:

    a. Identify high needs students in both academic and behavioral areas
    b. Select best practices for improvement
    c. Review Math and Reading deficits and design strategies and techniques

4. Refine behavioral/discipline procedure.
5. Develop professional training topics and literature review list for staff.
6. Utilize Clareen Einfeldt and Nancy Updegraff recommendations to identify improvement strategies.
7. Set a specific goal/target for ISAT performance improvement.
8. Post specific academic expectations in classrooms for each subject.
9. Middle School Focus - Orderly environment
10. Examine routines and rituals that (a) currently exist or (b) should exist in building, in classrooms, all group activities. Refine and develop appropriate ones for all school, classrooms, etc., i.e.:

    a. Single line on right side or left side when going to and from classroom.
    b. Use inside voices in building (describe inside voice - low tones, no yelling).
    c. Keep hands and feet to self (no touching others for any reason).
    d. Cafeteria rules.
    e. Develop plan for discussing with students, practicing with students, reminding students.

6. School-wide improvement focus area - select one area that will be top priority in building.
7. Applying Ritz Carlton model to customer service.
8. Making District Learning Agreement meaningful and doing necessary follow up actions with parents.

EXHIBIT G

Joliet Public Schools District 86
"The Ritz of Education"

The Joliet District 86 Mission Statement

Our schools, as partners with our children's parents and with the community, will create a safe and positive environment in which all students will learn and develop to their greatest potential. All students will be empowered to become lifelong learners, responsible citizens, and faring members of their communities.

The Joliet District 86 Credo

Joliet District 86 is a place where the genuine care and comfort of our learning community is our highest mission. We pledge to provide the finest education and facilities or our community in a warm, relaxed learning environment.

1. The Mission of District 86 represents what we believe. All stakeholders must know it, personalize it and let it govern their actions.
2. Our motto is, "We are Ladies and Gentlemen Serving Ladies and Gentlemen of all ages." As educational professionals, we must treat all of our students, guests and each other with respect and dignity.
3. A foundation of exceptional service to all stakeholders can be provided by following three simple steps of service:

    - Make everyone feel welcome and comfortable.
    - Anticipate a person's needs and be compliant with those needs.
    - Communicate with a positive attitude at all times.

4. The Employee Promise is the basis for our school work environments. It will be honored by all of our employees.
5. We support and encourage professional development for all of our employees.
6. The objectives of our school improvement plan and strategic plan are communicated and owned by everyone. It becomes each employee's responsibility to support them.
7. To create pride and joy in the workplace, all employees have the right to be involved in the planning of the work that affects them.
8. Each employee will identify and share defects or problems in the facility and/or operations of the school.
9. It is the responsibility of each employee to create a work environment of teamwork and lateral service so that the needs of our learning community are met.
10. Each employee is empowered to help solve problems. When a visitor, student or staff member has a problem or a special need, the employee should address and help resolve the issue.

Employee Promise

At our schools, our Ladies and Gentlemen are the most important resource we have. By applying the principles of trust, honesty, respect, integrity and commitment, we nurture and maximize talent to the benefit of each individual and each school. We also foster a work environment where diversity is valued, quality of life is enhanced, individual aspirations are fulfilled and the uniqueness of our schools are strengthened.

11. All Ladies and Gentlemen should take ownership for the cleanliness of the school property.
12. To provide the finest personal service, the learning community should take responsibility for identifying and meeting individual needs.
13. Never lose the opportunity to resolve a problem. Whoever receives a complaint will own it and help resolve it.
14. Smile - We are on stage. Always maintain positive eye contact. Use proper vocabulary with our learning community.

Use words such as:

- Good Morning
- Certainly
- I'll be happy to
- My pleasure

Do not use words such as:

- OK
- Sure
- Hi/Hello
- Folks
- No problem

15. Be an ambassador of your school in and outside of the workplace. Always speak positively. Communicate any concern to the appropriate person.
16. When possible, escort guests rather than pointing out directions to another area of the school or property.
17. Use "professional and courteous" telephone etiquette. Answer within three rings and with a "smile." Use the person's name when possible. When necessary, ask the caller, "May I place you on hold?" Adhere to voice mail standards.
18. Take pride in and care of your personal appearance. Everyone is responsible to convey a professional image by adhering to professional and proper clothing and grooming standards.
19. Think safety first. Each employee is responsible for creating a safe, secure and accident-free environment for everyone. Be aware of all fire and safety emergency procedures and report any security risks immediately.
20. Protecting the assets of the District is the responsibility of every employee and student. Conserve energy, properly maintain the facilities and protect the environment.

EXHIBIT H

“Ritz” Checklist

1. What will the Ritz approach look like in your building?

2. How will you monitor the implementation of the Ritz model?

3. What measurable outcomes will you use?

4. How will you display the “Ritz” strategies for all to see and use?

EXHIBIT I

Direction Questions

- ✓ Where do you want to be at the end of the year?
- ✓ How will you move your teachers to the great level?
- ✓ How will you articulate what you want the students to do?
- ✓ How will we measure teaching and learning in our building?
- ✓ What would it take to eliminate failure in your building?
- ✓ How will I open the hearts of teachers?
- ✓ What are the most important concepts/strategies that I will apply in the building?

EXHIBIT J

Discipline Expectations

In a Professional Learning Community, discipline procedures are fully in place. Students are taught the behaviors that are to be displayed and consequences clearly stated. Any discipline system put in place will incorporate rewards and positive reinforcement. All behavioral expectations are clearly communicated to parents and students and supported by staff. The following checklist is intended to serve as a guide for discipline procedures:

1. What is the Discipline model used by your school?
2. How have you shared all information regarding positive rewards and consequences and behavioral expectations with:

____Parents
____Students
____Staff

3. What interventions are in place in your building to direct student behaviors?
4. What analysis have you done of all activities and practices in your building that affect student behavior? What were your findings and what changes did you put in place based on your findings?
5. What research and literature have you used to assist with your development of discipline procedures?
6. What outcome measures will you use to ensure that your discipline procedures are effective?
7. What training has been provided for staff to ensure consistency in your use of discipline methods?
8. What discipline strategies do you use and what is t e source for these strategies?

9. What methods have you utilized to garner parental support for school rules and responses to behavior?
10. How often do you review your practices and procedures so that needed changes occur?
11. What additional resources are needed to implement your discipline program?

EXHIBIT K

Principal Self Evaluation Form
2008 - 2009 School Year

Name:________________________ School:________________________

DISTRICT GOAL: ALL CHILDREN WILL READ AT OR ABOVE GRADE LEVEL BY EIGHTH GRADE.

Reading at or above grade level

<u>Evidence:</u>

A) ISAT Improvement (Three year comparison) of students meeting or exceeding state standards in reading.

2006____ % 2007__% 2008____ %

B) Grade level progress for eighth grade students based upon ThinkLink Reading Assessment scores.

Percentage of Students	September 2008	November 2008	February 2009	May 2009
Exceeds Standards				
Meets Standards				
Below Standards				

C) Programs/Services/Interventions available at building level (Please list)

D) Staff participation in professional development for reading Please list sessions provided and number in attendance.

Sessions provided	Number in Attendance

EXHIBIT L

Principal Focus Activities

Junior High Principals	Elementary Principals
1. Weekly grade level parent meetings conducted by Academic Advisors	1. Increase focus on reading skills - Kindergarten – 2nd grade; 3rd grade remediation
a. Focused on weekly goals, requirements of student, support needed from parent	2. Relationship building
2. Develop specific follow-up plan for services for students with low GPA's	a. Student/Teacher
a. Written information for parents	b. Principal/Student - Greeting each student
b. Parental contact via phone	3. Individual Student Progress
3. Business work models applied to classroom practices.	4. Business Link with existing Partnership business
4. Business link forming partnerships with businesses	5. Monthly career exploration - bringjng in speakers to describe skills needed and job description
5. Monthly career exploration - bringing in speakers to describe skills needed and job description	6. Improving quality of instruction. Use of worksheets.
6. Improving quality of instruction address overuse of worksheets	

7. Weekly meetings with administrative team to establish focus and direction 8. Develop list of expectations building values for discussion sharing monitoring at all building staff a. Identify essential elements for building success. Distribute to all staff.	

All Principals

1. After school programs - ensuring participation of targeted students

    a. Develop Communication plan for parents

2. Increasing Parental Involvement

    a. Parent Resource Information
    b. Parent inservices
    c. Newsletter tips
    d. Web Page - monthly updates

5. Institute Days focused on teaching reading
6. Peace Builders/Peace Initiative - Provide overview of building activities
7. Joliet Reads Initiative - Provide overview
8. District Goals
9. Review of Student reading levels
10. Increasing reading minutes for targeted students (see chart)
11. Creating a professional environment

    a. Professional dress
    b. Literature discussion/Book Studies

3. Continued reduction of suspension/expulsion numbers through use of appropriate behavior management systems, student reminders, providing teacher inservice in areas such as classroom management, multicultural understandings
4. Classroom displays of strategic plan goals and School Improvement Plan actions, District Mission, Beliefs, Values
5. Building, hallway, lunchroom displays of school language posters, priming words, behavioral expectations, etc.
6. Building walk-throughs
7. Building and classroom cleanliness
8. District Learning Agreement (for all schools except magnet schools)

9. Student articulation

    a. Purpose of school
    b. Individual goals
    c. Career choice buttons

4. Goal setting activities
5. Differentiated Instruction implementation
6. Team planning-provide schedule/participant names

    a. Grade Level Teams
    b. Intervention Team
    c. Reading Committee
    d. Peace Committee
    e. Technology Committee
    f. Building Leadership Team

7. Read Star Principal characteristics - Identify self-improvement areas
8. Identify elements of success building will ascribe to
9. Utilize self-evaluation measures - ISAT performance data, Star Principal characteristics, reading and math levels for all students
10. Ongoing professional reading (from District list or self-selected)
11. Develop self-assessment activities for teachers based on analysis of available data, Star Teacher, and classroom expectations from Curriculum Department
12. Technology as it supports instruction
13. Compare your characteristics to those of successful principals in From Good to Great Schools

EXHIBIT M

Classroom Rounds (Walkthroughs): 10 Questions

In the Wilson County School District in North Carolina teams of district and school leaders, including the superintendent, visit classrooms regularly to observe and measure the effectiveness of teaching. Ten guiding questions shape their observations and group discussion:'

1. What is the Teacher doing?
2. What is the teacher saying and to whom?
3. What are the students doing?
4. What are the students saying and to whom?
5. What kind of student work is in view? Where?
6. Are students engaged?
7. What evidence shows that instruction is informed by prelesson student performance diagnostic data?
8. What evidence exists that instruction is adjusted to reflect the level of student skill and knowledge?
9. What evidence exists that the appropriate standard course of study is being taught?
10. Is the instructional objective posted or otherwise known to the students?

Source: AASA Leadership for Change

EXHIBIT N

Teacher Description

There Are Only Phenomenal Teachers In District 86

Phenomenal teachers:

- ✓ Accept the fact that many aspects of their students' lives are outside of their control.
- ✓ Realize that during the school day they ha e numerous opportunities to plant positive messages and foster seeds o resiliency in their students.
- ✓ Make choices every day to offer their students both academic and personal tools for success.
- ✓ Have high expectations and assist students in rising to the level of those expectations.
- ✓ Strive to convince students they can use education to improve the quality of their lives.
- ✓ Recognize that their students arrive at school with valuable cultural capital (no matter how much it differs from the values of mainstream society) that can be put to use in the classroom.

Question: Who are your phenomenal teachers? List them.

Gail L. Thompson, Through Ebony Eyes: What Teachers Need to Know But Are Afraid to Ask About African American Students, p.131

"What Great Teachers Do Differently"

1. Great teachers never forget that it is people, not programs that determine the quality of a school.
2. Great teachers establish clear expectations at the start of the year and follow them consistently as the year progresses.
3. When a student misbehaves, great teachers have on goal: to keep that behavior from happening again.
4. Great teachers have high expectations for: students but even higher expectations for themselves.
5. Great teachers know who is the variable in the classroom: They are. Good teachers consistently strive to improve, and they focus on something they can control - their own performance.
6. Great teachers create a positive atmosphere in their classrooms and schools. They treat every person with respect. In particular, they understand the power of praise.

- Fourteen Things That Matter Most by Todd Whitaker

EXHIBIT O

School Characteristics

What Does A Great School Look Like?

1. It is a place where staff members collaborate with others. We need partners to help us do our work. Yes__ No__
2. It is a place with an "almost stoic determination to do whatever needs to be done to make the school great" (p.20 Good to Great). Yes__No_
3. It is a place "infected with an incurable need to produce results" (p.30 Good to Great). Yes___No___
4. It is a place where the right people are on the bus. Yes___ No___
5. It is a place where obstacles are viewed as challenges to overcome. No excuses are made. Yes___No___
6. It is a place where staff members own responsibility for the children. The children are viewed as "ours" not as "those" children. Yes__ No__

Commonalities of Spotlight School

- Exemplary principals who are leaders of learning, who are resourceful, who craft a culture of high expectations, and who model leadership daily. Yes___No___
- A hard working, devoted staff that has the highest expectations, demands excellence, and REALLY believes each student can succeed. Yes___ No___
- Early literacy programs that focus on prevention and early intervention. Yes___No___
- Policies, programs, and services to include parents in the school and to educate parents in both parenting and in academic skills. Yes___No___
- Access to good nutrition and health care for all students. Yes___No___
- School-wide professional development on a single topic related to school improvement planning. Yes___No___

Quoted from Glenn McGee, "Closing Illinois' Achievement Gap: Lessons from the Golden Spike Schools"

About the Spotlight Schools

The Illinois Spotlight Schools awards grew out of research on high poverty, high performing schools funded by the Illinois State Board of Education and conducted at Northern Illinois University (NIU). One of the recommendations of that study was to establish a recognition program for these extraordinary schools. The Illinois school accountability system, which is aligned with "No Child Left Behind," requires rewards for high achieving schools as well as sanctions for schools that are not doing well. When NIU proposed development of an awards program for high poverty, high performing schools, ISBE agreed. Using criteria developed jointly, ISBE identified 26 Spotlight Schools, the first annual winners, in mid-October, 2003. ·

http://www.p20.niu.edu/P20/spotlightschools/schools.shtml

Newmann and Wehlage's decade long study of 1,200 schools found that high-performing schools had the following Characteristics:

1. Clear and shared purpose and goals.
2. Collaborative activity around a stated purpose.
3. Collective commitment to the success of all students.

EXHIBIT P

Reference List

Slocumb, Paul	*Boys In Crisis*
Streshly, William	*From Good To Great Schools: What Their Principals Do Well*
Whittaker, Todd	*Dealing With Difficult Parents*
Carney, Stephen	*The At-Risk Student In Our Schools*
Bell, Larry	*12 Powerful Words*
Dufour, Richard	*Professional Learning Communities at Work*
Tatum, Alfred	*Teaching Reading To Black Adolescent Males*
Steffy, Betty	*The Three Minute Classroom Walk-Through*
Marretta, Teresa	*Practical Approaches For Teaching Reading and Writing in Middle School*
Colorosa, Barbara	*The Bully, The Bullied, and the Bystander*
Pollack, William	*Real Boys*
Breaux, Annette	*Seven Simple Secrets: What The Best Teachers Know and Do*
Hale, Janice	*Black Children: Their Roots, Culture, and Learning Styles*

EXHIBIT Q

Partners In Learning

Student-Parent-Teacher-Administrator Agreement

We know that students learn best at ____________________________ School when everyone works together to encourage learning and practice appropriate behavior. This agreement is a promise to work together as a team to help ____________________________ achieve in school. Together, we can improve teaching and learning.

As a student, I pledge to

- ☐ work as hard as I can on mv school assignments.
- ☐ discuss with my parents what I am learning in school.
- ☐ respect myself, my family members, and school staff members.
- ☐ practice the goals or the District Behavior Standard at all times.
- ☐ ask my teacher questions when I don't understand something.
- ☐ use my public or school library frequently
- ☐ limit my TV watching and make time for reading.
- ☐ follow bus safety rules.

Student signature____________________________

As a parent, I pledge to

- ☐ encourage good study habits, including quiet study time at home.
- ☐ talk with my child every day about his or her school activities.
- ☐ reinforce respect for se lf and others.

- support the District Behavior Standards and review bus safety roles with my child.
- beware or my child's progress in school by attending conferences, reviewing school work and calling the teacher or school with questions.
- volunteer for my child's school or district.
- encourage good reading habits by reading to or with my child and by reading myself.
- limit my child's TV viewing and help select worthwhile programs.
- participate in at least 3 parent sessions during the school year.

Parent signature ______________________

As a teacher, I pledge to

- provide motivating and interesting learning experiences in my classroom.
- explain my instructional goals and grading system to students and parents.
- explain academic and classroom expectations to students and parents.
- provide for two-way communication with parents about what children are learning in school and how families can enhance children's learning at home and in the community.
- respect the uniqueness of my students and their families.
- teach and reinforce the District Behavior Standards, bus safety rules, and class expectations at all times.
- explore what techniques and materials help each child learn best.
- guide students and parents in choosing reading materials and TV programs

Teacher signature________________________________

As a principal/school administrator, I pledge to

- make sure students and parents feel welcome in school.
- communicate the school's mission and goals to students and parents.
- offer a variety of ways for families to be partners in their children's learning and to support this school.
- ensure a safe and nurturing learning environment.
- implement and promote the District Behavior Standards, bus safety rules, and school expectations at, all times.
- strengthen the partnership among students, parents, and teachers.
- act as the instructional leader by supporting teachers in their classrooms.
- provide opportunities for learning and development to teachers, families, and community members,

Principal signature ______________________________

Most importantly, we promise to help each other carry out this agreement.

Signed on this________________ day of__________________, 2008.

EXHIBIT R

Compañeros en el Aprendizaje

Contrato de Estudiantes-Padres- Maestros(as)-Administradores

Nosotros sabemos que los estudiantes aprenden mejor en la Escuela cuando todos trabajamos juntas con entusiasmo para aprender y practicar la conducta apropiada. Este contrato es una promesa de trabajar unidos como un equipo para ayudar a a triunfar en la escuela. Juntos podemos mejorar la enseñanza y el aprendizaje.

Como estudiante, Yo prometo

- trabajar con gran entusiasmo en mis tareas escolares.
- hablar con mis padres de lo que estoy aprendiendo en la escuela.
- respetarme a mí mismo/a respetar a mi familia, y a miembros de la facultad escolar.
- practicar las metas de las Normas de Comportamiento del Distrito todo el tiempo.
- preguntar a mi maestro/a cuando yo no entiendo algo.
- usar la biblioteca pública o de la escuela con frecuencia.
- limitar mi tiempo para ver televisión y tomar más tiempo para leer
- seguir las reglas de seguridad del autobús.

Firma del estudiante______________________

Como padre, Yo prometo

- apoyar los buenos hábitos para estudiar, incluyendo tiempo para estudiar en casa.

☐ hablar con mi hijo/a diario de sus actividades escolares.

☐ reafirmar el respeto por sí mismo/a y por los demás.

☐ apoyar las Normas de Comportamiento del Distrito y las reglas de seguridad del autobús con mi hijo/a.

☐ estar al pendiente del progreso de mi hijo/a en la escuela, asistiendo a conferencias, revisando el trabajo de la escuela, y llamando a los maestros/as o a la escuela si tengo preguntas.

☐ ofrecerme como voluntario/a en la escuela de mi hijo/a o distrito.

☐ adoptar buenos hábitos de lectura y leer con mi hijo/a.

☐ limitar el tiempo que mi hijo/a ve televisión y ayudarlo a seleccionar buenos programas.

☐ participar en tres juntas de padres durante el año escolar.

Firma del padre____

Como Maestro(a), Yo prometo

☐ proporcionar experiencias interesantes de aprendizaje que motiven a los estudiantes en mi salón de clases.

☐ explicar mis metas de instrucci6n y el sistema de calificaciones a los estudiantes y a los padres.

☐ explicar a los estudiantes y padres lo que se espera académicamente y las reglas del sal6n de clases.

☐ proporcionar un medio de comunicaci6n recíproca con los padres acerca de lo que sus niños/as están aprendiendo en la escuela, y de qué manera las familias los pueden ayudar a aprender más en casa y en la comunidad.

☐ respetar la individualidad de mis estudiantes y sus familias.

☐ enseñar y reafirmar las Normas de Comportamiento del Distrito, las reglas de seguridad del autobús, y las metas de la clase todo el tiempo

☐ explorar el modo y los materiales que puedan ayudar para que cada niño/a aprenda mejor.

- guiar a los estudiantes y a sus padres a seleccionar materiales de lectura y programas de televisión

Firma del Maestro/a____

Como Director/Administrador de la Escuela, Yo prometo

- asegurarme de que los estudiantes y sus padres se sientan bienvenidos en la escuela.
- comunicar la misi6n y las metas de la escuela a los estudiantes y a sus padres.
- ofrecer varias maneras para que las familias puedan ser participantes dcl aprendizaje de sus hijos/as y apoyen a la escuela.
- ofrecer un ambiente de aprendizaje seguro y educativo.
- implementar y promover las Normas de Comportamiento del Distrito, las reglas de seguridad del autobús, y las metas de la escuela todo el tiempo.
- reforzar el compañerismo entre estudiantes, padres y maestros/as.
- actuar como el líder instruccional apoyando a los/as maestros/as en sus salones de clase.
- proporcionar oportunidades de aprendizaje y desarrollo para los maestros/as, las familias y los miembros de la comunidad.

Firma del Director/a________________________________

Y sobre todo, muy importante, nosotros prometemos ayudarnos los unos a los otros para cumplir este contrato.

Firmado el ______día de______, 2008

From Good Schools to 1 Great Schools

By Susan Penny Gray and William A. Streshly

Suggestions for Principals

Building Relationships

- Discover the strengths of each member of the staff.
- Develop meaningful relationship with each person encountered.
- Attempt to develop meaningful relationships with estranged or disengaged staff.
- Openly communicate with staff.

Promoting Teacher Leadership

- Involve staff in decision making. Promote collective capacity, eliminate teacher isolation.
- Promote leadership and professionalism.
- Organize and support professional learning communities.

Exhibiting Professional Will

- Be fearless.
- Act as a buffer between school and external forces.
- Be adamant.
- Voice priorities.

Exhibiting Personal Humility

- Be humble.
- Be self-effacing.
- Be quick to praise others.
- Be unassuming.

Exhibiting Compelling Modesty

- Downplay being I-centric and charismatic.
- Assign credit to others for success.
- Acknowledge the work of teachers as the reason for improved student performance.
- Minimize the part you play.

Accepting the Blame

- Accept blame for failures.
- At times, assign personal success to "luck."

Exercising Ambition for the School Before Ambition for Self

- Strive to see the school even more successful after you are gone.
- Encourage professionalism and leadership among staff.
- Value staff development.
- Offer assistance to your successor.

Promoting Competitive Staff

- Promote competitive spirit for the whole school.
- Select staff who are eager to see that the school is successful and willing to do whatever it takes to make that success happen.

Exhibiting Unwavering Resolve

- Be relentless and aggressive in working toward the mission and vision of the school.
- Be continuously involved with the primary operations of the school through committee work, classroom visitations, grade-level meetings, or department meetings.

Communicating the Resolve to Staff

- Be persuasive.
- Maintain and communicate the belief that something can and will be accomplished.
- Communicate clarity of purpose: a clear goal should be in sight at all times.
- Accept no excuses.

Getting the Right People

- To the maximum degree possible, maintain the latitude to hire and dismiss school staff.
- Be aggressive in your choices for teachers while staying within the rules and regulations of the district's hiring process.
- Clarify your vision with potential faculty from the beginning to foster a fit with school staff.
- Work with district personnel and other principals to refine the hiring process.

Working With the Right People

- Convince the staff who do not work well with the school program to transfer.
- Work with teachers who desire to improve and who have the capacity to improve.

Confronting the Brutal Facts

- With staff, analyze student achievement and demographic data.
- Study the culture of the school and community.

Solving the Dilemmas

- Develop an important vision for the school based on the facts.
- Work through sensitive challenges.

- Have faith that challenges will be overcome and communicate that faith to others.

Knowing What You Are Best At

- Know what teachers are best at (e.g., skill and determination) and support them.
- Continually strive for excellence in the one thing that distinguishes the school as great.

Knowing What Drives Your Educational Engine

- Determine what drives the educational engine of the school e.g., increase time spent teaching reading or increase time for students to read, or both).
- Reject programs and processes that detract the school and its teachers from driving the educational engine.

Being Passionate About It

- Live your passion every day.
- Be a fanatic about your school's educational engine.

Building a Culture Around the Ideas of Freedom and Responsibility

- Establish goals and a vision, and stay firm but not tyrannical about them.
- Encourage staff input and innovation.
- Emphasize collaboration.
- Encourage teacher freedom and responsibility within the agreed on goals and vision.

Filling the Culture With Self-Disciplined People

- Establish clear expectations.
- Hire staff who are disciplined, self-confident, focused, productive, and motivated to do what is necessary to promote student learning.

- Provide support for staff with materials, personnel, and staff development.

Adhering Consistently to the Hedgehog Concept

- Adhere to the three circles rule: Know what your school and staff is best at. Know what drives the educational engine of the school. Be passionate about it.

Building Trust

- Be honest.
- Be optimistic.
- Be considerate.
- Develop leadership among staff and, in doing so, display trust in their abilities.
- Foster a culture of trusted relationships among staff, students, and parents.

Promoting Participative Governance and Professional Learning Communities

- Provide opportunities for staff to play a significant role in: goal setting, problem solving, and making decisions that affect their work.
- Encourage openness in others.
- Facilitate effective communication.
- Encourage teacher involvement, eliminating issues of risk and threat.
- Shift thinking from a focus on teaching to a focus on learning.
- Use DuFour's (2005) three questions to engage conversation across the school:
  - How do we want each student to learn?
  - How will we know when each student has learned it?
  - How will we respond when a student experiences difficulty in learning?

Getting Into Classrooms Often

- Schedule dedicated time each day to visit classrooms.
- Focus on curriculum and instructional issues when visiting classrooms. Communicate this focus with teachers prior to visiting.'
- Make it clear to teachers your purpose for visiting, whether for formal or informal observations. Is your purpose to evaluate or to provide support?

EMPLOYEE

COMMITMENT

Interpersonal Relationships

We will be respectful, caring, supportive and helpful of each other. We will adhere to the District rules for student interactions:

a) **No arguing with students**
b) **No yelling at students**
c) No use of sarcasm with students

(Sarcasm is the cruel act of humiliating someone in front of their peers under the guise of humor.)

- Todd Whitaker

Performance

We will put forth our best effort to produce the highest quality product - well educated students. We will perform the duties, tasks and responsibilities for which we are paid.

Proficiency Requirements

We will continue to improve our skills and acquire new knowledge about our work.

District Filter

We will serve as ambassadors for the district by speaking positively about the place where we work. Any criticisms, or negative comments will be developed into specific actions and contributions you can make to help us be all that you would wish.

PARTNERS IN LEARNING

Student-Parent-Teacher-Administrator Agreement

We know that students learn best at ______________________________ School when everyone works together to encourage learning and practice appropriate behavior. This agreement is a promise to work together as a team to help ________________________________achieve in school. Together, we can improve teaching and learning.

As a **student, I pledge to**

- ☐ work as hard as I can on mv school assignments.
- ☐ discuss with my parents what I am learning in school.
- ☐ respect myself, my family members, and school staff members.
- ☐ practice the goals or the District Behavior Standard at all times.
- ☐ ask my teacher questions when I don't understand something.
- ☐ use my public or school library frequently
- ☐ limit my TV watching and make time for reading.
- ☐ follow bus safety rules.

Student signature____________________________

As a parent, I pledge to

- ☐ encourage good study habits, including quiet study time at home.
- ☐ talk with my child every day about his or her school activities.
- ☐ reinforce respect for se lf and others.
- ☐ support the District Behavior Standards and review bus safety roles with my child.
- ☐ beware or my child's progress in school by attending conferences, reviewing school work and calling the teacher or school with questions.

- volunteer for my child's school or district.
- encourage good reading habits by reading to or with my child and by reading myself.
- limit my child's TV viewing and help select worthwhile programs.
- participate in at least 3 parent sessions during the school year.

Parent signature ___________________________

As a teacher, I pledge to

- provide motivating and interesting learning experiences in my classroom.
- explain my instructional goals and grading system to students and parents.
- explain academic and classroom expectations to students and parents.
- provide for two-way communication with parents about what children are learning in school and how families can enhance children's learning at home and in the community.
- respect the uniqueness of my students and their families.
- teach and reinforce the District Behavior Standards, bus safety rules, and class expectations at all times.
- explore what techniques and materials help each child learn best.
- explore what techniques and materials help each child learn best
- guide students and parents in choosing reading materials and TV programs

Teacher signature_______________________________________

As a principal/school administrator, I pledge to

make sure students and parents feel welcome in school.
communicate the school's mission and goals to students and parents.

offer a variety of ways for families to be partners in their children's learning and to support this school.
ensure a safe and nurturing learning environment.
implement and promote the District Behavior Standards, bus safety rules, and school expectations at, all times.
strengthen the partnership among students, parents, and teachers.
act as the instructional leader by supporting teachers in their classrooms.
provide opportunities for learning and development to teachers, families, and community members,

Principal signature ______________________________

Mostly importantly, we promise to help each other carry out this agreement.

Signed on this________________ day of___________________, 2005.

Compañeros en el Aprendizaje

Contrato de Estudiantes-Padres- Maestros(as)-Administradores

Nosotros sabemos que los estudiantes aprenden mejor en la Escuela cuando todos trabajamos juntas con entusiasmo para aprender y practicar la conducta apropiada. Este contrato es una promesa de trabajar unidos como un equipo para ayudar a a triunfar en la escuela. Juntos podemos mejorar la enseñanza y el aprendizaje.

Como estudiante, Yo prometo

- trabajar con gran entusiasmo en mis tareas escolares.
- hablar con mis padres de lo que estoy aprendiendo en la escuela.
- respetarme a mí mismo/a respetar a mi familia, y a miembros de la facultad escolar.
- practicar las metas de las Normas de Comportamiento del Distrito todo el tiempo.
- preguntar a mi maestro/a cuando yo no entiendo algo.
- usar la biblioteca pública o de la escuela con frecuencia.
- limitar mi tiempo para ver televisión y tomar más tiempo para leer
- seguir las reglas de seguridad del autobús.

Firma del estudiante____________________

Como padre, Yo prometo

- apoyar los buenos hábitos para estudiar, incluyendo tiempo para estudiar en casa.
- hablar con mi hijo/a diario de sus actividades escolares.
- reafirmar el respeto por sí mismo/a y por los demás.
- apoyar las Normas de Comportamiento del Distrito y las reglas de seguridad del autobús con mi hijo/a.

- estar al pendiente del progreso de mi hijo/a en la escuela, asistiendo a conferencias, revisando el trabajo de la escuela, y llamando a los maestros/as o a la escuela si tengo preguntas.
- ofrecerme como voluntario/a en la escuela de mi hijo/a o distrito.
- adoptar buenos hábitos de lectura y leer con mi hijo/a.
- limitar el tiempo que mi hijo/a ve televisión y ayudarlo a seleccionar buenos programas.
- participar en tres juntas de padres durante el año escolar.

Firma del padre____

Como Maestro(a), Yo prometo

- proporcionar experiencias interesantes de aprendizaje que motiven a los estudiantes en mi salón de clases.
- explicar mis metas de instrucci6n y el sistema de calificaciones a los estudiantes y a los padres.
- explicar a los estudiantes y padres lo que se espera académicamente y las reglas del sal6n de clases.
- proporcionar un medio de comunicaci6n recíproca con los padres acerca de lo que sus niños/as están aprendiendo en la escuela, y de qué manera las familias los pueden ayudar a aprender más en casa y en la comunidad.
- respetar la individualidad de mis estudiantes y sus familias.
- enseñar y reafirmar las Normas de Comportamiento del Distrito, las reglas de seguridad del autobús, y las metas de la clase todo el tiempo
- explorar el modo y los materiales que puedan ayudar para que cada niño/a aprenda mejor.
- guiar a los estudiantes y a sus padres a seleccionar materiales de lectura y programas de televisión

Firma del Maestro/a____

Como Director/Administrador de la Escuela, Yo prometo

- ☐ asegurarme de que los estudiantes y sus padres se sientan bienvenidos en la escuela.
- ☐ comunicar la misi6n y las metas de la escuela a los estudiantes y a sus padres.
- ☐ ofrecer varias maneras para que las familias puedan ser participantes dcl aprendizaje de sus hijos/as y apoyen a la escuela.
- ☐ ofrecer un ambiente de aprendizaje seguro y educativo.
- ☐ implementar y promover las Normas de Comportamiento del Distrito, las reglas de seguridad del autobús, y las metas de la escuela todo el tiempo.
- ☐ reforzar el compañerismo entre estudiantes, padres y maestros/as.
- ☐ actuar como el líder instruccional apoyando a los/as maestros/as en sus salones de clase.
- ☐ proporcionar oportunidades de aprendizaje y desarrollo para los maestros/as, las familias y los miembros de la comunidad.

Firma del Director/a____

Y sobre todo, muy importante, nosotros prometemos ayudarnos los unos a los otros para cumplir este contrato.

Firmado el _______día de_______, 2005

Self-Reflection Questions:

1. Are you the "right" person on the "right" bus?
2. Do you support the work of others or are you a "naysayer"?
3. Are you self-motivated?
4. Are you self-disciplined?
5. Are you making a contribution?
6. Are you doing the job for which you are paid?
7. Is your work a mission, and not just a job?
8. Are you finding ways to continuously improve the way you do your work?
9. Do you conduct yourself as a professional? (Professional is a way of acting and looking, not just how many degrees you have.)
10. Do you own the children we serve?
11. Do you show respect to all in your environment?
12. Have you planned how your work will occur?
13. Do you have a self-improvement plan?
14. Have you faced the brutal truth about your work and then moved forward to make things better?
15. Do you have the desire to be great at what you do?
16. Do you follow the plan in place or are you doing your own thing?
17. Are you part of the school team? The District team?
18. Are you on the same path as everyone else or have you gone down a different path?

Principals' Information Handbook

Materials provided by:
Dr. Phyllis M. Wilson
October 2002

Table of Contents

District Focus for 2002 – 2003

Goal: To refine our work

I. By creating a learning community.
II. By establishing a positive building climate (School Survey).
III. By integrating data analysis, best practice, and research into the decision making process.
IV. By implementing programs and services proven to work.
V. By developing strategies to accomplish goals.
VI. By using star principal, star teacher, and star employee characteristics to measure performance.
VII. By displaying a positive attitude.
VIII. By adhering to concepts in No Excuses, Results and district "Finished Product" from the Facilities Plan.
IX. By prominently displaying district goals, behavioral expectations, mission and values statements throughout the building.
X. By establishing student ambassador program.
XI. By involving parents and community members in the educational process.

District Goals

FOR
2002 – 2003

Elementary Level

GOAL I: All students will read at or above grade level by third grade.

GOAL II: All students will meet or exceed state math standards for third and fifth grades.

Junior High Level

GOAL I: All sixth grade students will read at or above grade level by seventh grade.

GOAL II: All eighth grade students will be prepared for high school English placement at or above grade level.

GOAL III: All students will meet or exceed state math standards for eighth grade.

GOAL IV: All eighth grade students will be assigned to Algebra I in ninth grade.

Points to Remember

1. Instruction should occur at the highest level, not the lowest level.
2. Teacher has the responsibility for determining what the low performing student does not know and needs to know and provide this information by:

   a) Direct instruction to student.
   b) Referral to after school, before school tutoring, other remedial sources in school, and in the community via "Student Instruction Plan."
   c) Self-reflection on areas of disconnect with distinct student populations. Participation in efficacy and training strand will help in this area.

4. Principal needs to deliver a clear message to students that:
   a) Disrespecting staff is not acceptable and will be dealt with.

      1. Define disrespect for students.
      2. By identifying consequences on a periodic basis with students as a reminder.
      3. By posting of consequences from student handbook around building.
      4. By posting school rules at visible points to serve as cues and reminders for students.
      5. By periodic reminders to parents via verbal and written means.
      6. By conversations with students emphasizing their responsibility as students to place academics as the highest priority during the time they are in school.
      7. By linking with a community agency to develop joint plans for most disruptive students and their families.

Star Principal Ideology

- ☆ For any real learning to occur, the safety and security of everyone in and around the school building is an absolute prerequisite.
- ☆ Teachers are not here to help me be a principal. I am here to help them improve student's learning.
- ☆ To improve the learning of impoverished student, student and their families must be connected to health and human services.
- ☆ I am paid more than teachers not because I am smarter, work harder, and the best educator, or hold a state license as an administrator. I am paid more because I am accountable and responsible for the effectiveness of the total school.
- ☆ Teachers who can control their classes are not necessarily good teachers. Classroom management is a necessary but insufficient condition. Student learning is the criterion for deciding teachers' "goodness".
- ☆ Parents are not the consumers of education; society is. The role of parents is not simply to have things explained to them. Parents are sources of useful information about their children, resources in the educational process, and partners in meeting the needs of students.
- ☆ Everyone who sets foot in this school must be treated as if he or she were important dignitary.
- ☆ Leadership means helping people demand what is in their best interests rather than acceding to whatever they want.
- ☆ Admitting shortcomings of the school program is the first step toward resolving weaknesses; I must never stonewall or cover up.
- ☆ There is no greater benefit to the school than removing an ineffectual teacher. No matter how lengthy, costly, or time consuming the process, it must be pursued to completion.
- ☆ To be accountable for instruction, I must be involved in the selection and assignment of new teachers.
- ☆ There is nothing of any importance that I can decide completely on my own.

It is my job to protect this school from the chaos in which we must operate. Despite state mandates, school board politics, temporary superintendent, and central office turf wars, I can keep this school focused on the kids and their educational needs.

Star Teacher Characteristics

1. Establish at least four rules at the beginning of each year.
2. Believe that problems are part of their job and are proactive disciplinarians.
3. Invest time and efforts creating learning activities that have helped them build caring relationships with each of the children.
4. View discipline primarily as a natural consequence of their ability to interest and involve learners.
5. See themselves as working with students, coaching, and providing help.
6. Use the class as a group to set norms of expected behavior.
7. Use homework to create assignments that youngsters are able to do independently and successfully.
8. Describe parental support in terms of parents showing an interest in what their children do in school and providing them with basics such as privacy, safety, sleep, nutrition, and health care.
9. Do not blame parents.
10. Base evaluation primarily on student effort.
11. Teach in units that frequently involve team or collaborative learning.
12. Conceive that their primary goal is turning kids on to learning – i.e., engaging them in becoming independent learners.
13. Believe all youngsters should learn as much as they can from as broad and varied a curriculum as possible.
14. Believe in the intrinsic value of learning.
15. Are lifelong learners of various subjects, skills, and fields of study?
16. Believe it is their responsibility to find ways of engaging their students in learning.
17. Interest their children in learning by modeling their own interest in learning.
18. Always choose the children over the system.
19. Have two clear goals and persist toward them: First, if the children are deeply involved in a valuable learning activity, it is the teacher's job to keep it going. Second, it is their job to patiently, courteously, and professionally persist and negotiate with the principal.
20. Have culturally relevant teaching practices.

Principal Tasks for Star Teacher Development

1. Develop list that identifies key characteristics of star teachers.
2. Identify teachers on staff who exhibit these characteristics.
3. Identify how you will reward / highlight the display of star skills.
4. Identify teachers on staff who do not exhibit star teacher characteristics.
5. Identify how you will assist these teachers?
6. Identify the expectations you hold for Teachers? Students? Parents?
7. Identify what needs to be in place so that your expectations are met.

Star Teacher Rubric

		Weak	Basic	Proficient	Strong
STAR TEACHERS EXHIBIT THE FOLLOWING:		Little or no evidence of the outcome	Beginning of or some evidence of the outcome	Detailed, consistent evidence of the outcome	Highly creative, mature presence of outcome
CURRICULUM All assignments are special and must be meaningful. Give non-traditional homework. Are suspicious of direct instruction. Use various materials to elicit student interest. Achieve real learning in low-income schools by the project method. Adept at the project method and where children are in the continuum of readiness for project learning.					
CLIMATE Interested in effort not ability. Move students into internal commitments. Know that learning is enjoyable. Reach every individual personally several times every month. Building trusting, warm, loving respectful relationships. Develop intrinsic learning in students. Create independent learners who don't need them. Determine what to focus on and what to ignore. Teach the concept that trying and making mistakes is normal. Believe success is associated with effort, not chance. Believe it is their responsibility to interest and engage children in wanting to learn. Convince each child that he is needed and important. Have fantastic attendance in their classrooms. Join with children in the learning adventure.					

CLASS COMMUNITY See their job as creating a safe haven where violence does not intrude. Use punishments as a last resort. Use the class as a group to set norms of expected behavior. Use the group as a restraining force. Discipline through learning activities. Use logical consequences. Don't think in terms of rewards and punishments. Sensitive to rules and policies. Set up few rules with logical consequences.					
		Weak	Basic	Proficient	Strong
STAR TEACHERS EXHIBIT THE FOLLOWING:		Little or no evidence of the outcome	Beginning of or some evidence of the outcome	Detailed, consistent evidence of the outcome	Highly creative, mature presence of outcome
COMMUNITY Know parental support means parents show an interest in what their children do. Believe most parents are, or (if approached in terms of what they can do) will be active cooperative parents. Work with parents rather than try to supervise them. Want to learn about children's out-of-school lives.					
COMMITMENT Are persistent. Are lifelong learners. Reflective. Have great emotional stamina. Have physical stamina. Have endless interest in what they are doing. Have extraordinary managerial skills. Develop support networks.					

Rewards for staff

Keeping in mind the internal motivation and commitment above, the following may be rewards for staff who display star qualities:

Workshop opportunities

Mini grant funds to spend as they see the need

Observation of other teachers

Letter of praise sent to the superintendent

Developing stars

In encouraging others to become stars, the best method is selecting stars from the beginning. Other ways to develop talent is non-stars are listed below:

1. Maximize learning time – time on task
   a. Routines, many and automatic
   b. Limit rues with natural consequences
2. High expectations
   a. Assume responsibility for student assessment
   b. Prepare students to these expectations
3. Student accountability
   a. Feedback on homework.
   b. Focus on process not the product.
4. Questioning skill
   a. Open-ended
   b. Student driven

BUILDING A
NO EXCUSES
LEARNING ENVIRONMENT
Joliet Public Schools District 86
2001 - 2002

What is a "No Excuses" Learning Environment?

A place that refuses to make poverty an excuse for academic failure.	A place where principals are skilled in finding training, and bringing out the best in teachers.	A place that ensures that all children master key subjects, especially reading, math, and fluency in the English language.
A place that has safe, orderly and happy environment	A place where students, of all races and income levels are held to high standards and expectations.	A place that tests constantly to determine whether each and every child is learning.
A place where parents actively support the educational process	A place that ensures that all children succeed.	A place where teachers are held to the same high standards they hold students
	A place that recognizes that some children may learn at different paces	

How will we Measure our Success?

By making continuous improvement in assessment results

By eliminating any excuses made for poor student performance

By demonstration of student skills, knowledge, and writing capabilities.

By analyzing ISAT **test results.**

By analyzing CAT/5 test results

By reading and math level placements.

Fish Philosophy

Taken from: **Fish** by Stephen C. Lundin, Ph.d., Harry Paul, and John Christensen.

Choose your attitude – bring your best self to work and love the work you do. There is always a choice about the way you do your work, even if there is not a choice about the work itself.

You can be serious about business and still play – have fun with the way you conduct business. Have a good time but do so in a respectful manner. Engage other people and welcome them to join in the fun.

Make Their Day – look for as many ways as you can to create great memories. You create great memories whenever you make someone's day. Serving our customers well will give us the satisfaction that comes to those who serve others.

Be Present – Listen well to the person in front of you and do not allow yourself to be distracted. Show consideration for the other person.

There is always a choice about the way you do your work, even if there is not a choice about the work itself.

OUR WORKPLACE

As you enter this place of work please *choose* to make today a great day. Your colleagues, customers, team members, and you yourself will be thankful. Find ways to *play.* We can be serious about our work without being serious about ourselves. Stay focused in order to *be present* when your customers and team members most need you. And should you feel your energy lapsing, try this surefire remedy: Find someone who needs a helping hand, a word of support, or a good ear – and *make their day.*

FISH by: Stephen C. Lunden, Ph.D.,

Harry Paul and John Christenson

District Assessment Description

There are two types of assessment used in District 86. They are:

Criterion Referenced –

1. **Measurement to know whether students are proficient in the standards and knowledge we value.**

   Norm Referenced –

2. **Measurement of how our students compare to other students across the nation.**

Based on the district's vision, mission statement, and goals, a profile was developed of the kind of skills the district wished to be displayed by students. Those skills were identified as follows:

Educational Expectations for District 86 Students:

Our "Finished Product"

- Reading, writing and math skills at or above grade level
- Responsible citizenship
- Life-long learners
- Contributing, caring community members
- Prepared for a rigorous High School curriculum
- Appropriate social skills
- Capable of articulating educational purpose and their contribution to academic success
- Technologically literate
- Students developing to their greatest potential.

Joliet Public Schools District 86

Our schools, as partners with our children's parents and with the community, will create a safe and positive environment in which all students will learn and develop to their greatest potential. All students will be empowered to become lifelong learners, responsible citizens, and caring members of their communities.

Students

We believe all students can learn and are entitled to an equitable education which ensures quality, nurtures self-esteem, and allows students to reach their greatest potential.

Employees

We believe that effective schools have employees who embody the vision and mission of the school district and are committed to providing an equitable and quality education for all children

Joliet Public Schools District 86

Board

We believe that effective schools have a School Board which provides an equitable and quality education for all children through its leadership and commitment to the community.

Parents

We believe that effective schools have parents whose active involvement in the educational process supports their children and the school community.

Com m unity

We believe the quality of life in a community depends on the education of its citizens. We believe the quality of schools depends on the financial and human resources provided by its community.

will be assigned to Algebra I in ninth grade.

I want people who walk into every building in the district to receive the clear message that we are serious about the business of academics. This opinion should be formed because they see:

- Students moving quietly through the halls

- Teachers/students and students/students interacting respectfully and positively with each other

- Students completing work assignments and remaining on task

- Students articulating their goals and reason for being in school

1. Every building will have a safe and orderly environment.

    A. There are posted guides for behavioral expectations.
    B. Students are taught the behaviors staff wishes them to display.
    C. Everyone in the school assumes responsibility for student behavior.

2. There is an articulated, consistent approach to discipline.

    A. Principles of Discipline with Dignity are practiced.
    B. Focus is on changing behavior to a self-monitoring, internalized approach.

3. Quality instruction occurs in every classroom.

    A. Professional development and literature review occurs to improve skills.
    B. Instructional planning occurs.
    C. Continuous feedback is given to students regarding effort and improvement actions.
    D. Everyone is on task.
    E. Teachers are teaching and students are learning.
    F. Multiple strategies are utilized - engaged learning, differentiated instruction.

4. High expectations are held by everyone.

    A. Belief in students ability to learn (effort versus ability thinking).
    B. Student success is highest priority.

5. Professional climate is created.

    A. Colleagues help and support each other.
    B. Learning dialogue occurs - what can I do to get better? What new knowledge can be shared?
    C. Staff knows district mission, goals, priorities, focus, expectations and incorporates them into their work.
    D. Accepts responsibility for representing school and district in all that is done.

Building will ensure:

6. Staff will:
    a. Know District's Mission
    b. Know District's Goal
    c. Participate in staff development activities
    d. Read professional literature
    e. Create a professional environment – dialogue, dress

Other Superintendent's Standards

- Interpersonal Interactions
- Performance Level
- Professional Knowledge

I. Interpersonal Relationships

A. We will be respectful, and helpful to will adhere to the district rules for student interactions:

1) No arguing with students.
2) No yelling at students.
3) No use of sarcasm with students.

(Sarcasm is the cruel act of humiliating someone in front of their peers under the guise of humor.)

III. Proficiency

Requirements

A. We will continue to improve our skills and acquire new knowledge about our work.

IV. District Filter

A. We will serve as ambassadors for the district by speaking positively about the place where we work. Any criticisms, or negative comments will be developed into specific actions and contributions you can make to help us be all that you would wish.

Reflective Questions

1. Given the Superintendent's Standards, what does this mean for Students, Staff and Parents of your school?
2. What challenges exist to fully implement the Superintendent's Standards?
3. Are the standards similar/dissimilar to your own?

General Questions

1. What are the standards that exist at your school?
2. Do you agree/disagree with the existing standards?
3. What standards would you like to see in place at your school?
4. Name three ways you "own" the student behaviors at your school?
5. Name three things you do to improve your capabilities?

Joliet Public Schools District 86
What is a "No Excuses" Learning Environment?

I. Instructional Quality

A. Rigorous Academics (compacted curriculum accelerated learning)
B. Differentiated Instruction
C. Reading Emphasis
D. Basic Skills Proficiency - ability to read, write, compute
E. Interpersonal Relationships

1) Children for Peace
2) School Language

II. Parent Connections

A. Learning Agreement
B. Student Handbook - Rights and Responsibilities
C. Parent Sessions
D. Communication Techniques

1) Newsletter
2) Brochures
3) Guided Conferences
4) Letters

1. Posting in every classroom, a one page overview of school improvement plan.
2. Posting in every classroom, a one page overview of district strategic plan to focus work.
3. Having students articulate the purpose of school.
4. Distributing at conferences, parent packets indicating how parents can support learning process.
5. Applying learning benchmarks for each grade level.
6. Adhering to the district priorities for staff trainings - Dr. Ruby Payne's Framework for Understanding Poverty, differentiated instruction.
7. Holding high expectations for employees as well as students.
8. Developing self-selected goals for students and staff.
9. Reviewing weekly student work samples.
10. Posting of district goals, mission statement, and beliefs.
11. Increased emphasis on reading.
12. Continuing use of data to inform instruction.
13. Developing a student book club.
14. Implementing reading initiatives.
15. Disseminating learning agreements for parents for all schools.

1. Student articulation.
    a. Knowing purpose of why they are in school.
    b. Knowing reading and math levels.
    c. Setting goals daily and weekly.
    d. Student scripting to describe learning environment and connect with others.
    e. Describing plans for the future- career choice button.

Determining What Is Effective?
What Is The Purpose?

Will This Actually Accomplish The Purpose?

How Will The Most Positive And Productive People Feel About This?

Question

How can we change instruction to better meet needs of students? Versus how can we change students so that instruction will fit?

Schmoker suggestion:
Principals should be reminding staff of why they are there with "boorish redundancy."

Anisha Erkins and Anthony Stallings - Third Grade, Farragut School

- You cannot teach a child you do not love.
- You cannot teach a child you do not respect.
- You cannot teach a child you do not understand.

1. Increase time on task.
2. Increase student engagement.
3. Determine minimum time on core areas.
4. Analyze the current time spent on core areas.
5. Realign the purpose of noncore areas.
6. Change school schedule to give priority to core areas.
7. Increase length of the day.
8. Increase length of the year.
9. Require regular, consistent, quality homework.
10. Establish nonschool tutorial programs.
11. Focus the curriculum

A. Use a standards-based approach.
B. Align vertical curriculum.
C. Increase graduation requirements.
D. Introduce weighted grades.
E. Introduce harder subjects earlier.
F. Prevent regression to easier subjects.
G. Eliminate grade inflation.
H. Teach what is tested and test what is taught.
I. Modify practices that lower student achievement.

THE NEXT LEVEL:

FOR ACADEMIC ACHIEVEMENT

Joliet Public Schools District 86

Table of Contents

District Mission

Our schools, as partners with our children's parents and with the community, will create a safe and positive environment in which all students will learn and develop to their greatest potential All students will be empowered to become lifelong learners, responsible citizens, and caring members of their communities.

Students

We believe all students can learn and are entitled to an equitable education which ensures quality, nurtures self-esteem, and allows students to reach their greatest potential.

Employees

We believe that effective schools have employees who embody the vision and mission of the school district and *are* committed to providing an equitable and quality education for all children.

Board

We believe that effective schools have a School Board which provides an equitable and quality education for all children through its leadership and commitment to the community.

Parents

We believe that effective schools have parents whose active involvement in the educational process supports their children and the school community.

Community

We believe the quality of life in a community depends on the education of its citizens. We believe the quality of schools depends on the financial and human resources provided by its community.

District 86 Value Statement

"In District 86, we value academic achievement through equitable access to a quality education."

Core Values

- Achievement
- Equity
- Quality Education

Definitions

- Academic Achievement - child centered decisions accompanied by appropriate instructional strategies that demonstrate student performance.
- Equitable - Providing needed educational resources and materials based on identified student needs.
- Quality - Effective as measured by academic improvement of students and professional growth of staff.

District Goals

Revised July 2006

Elementary Level

GOAL I:	All students will read at or above grade level by third grade as measured by ThinkLink Learning Predictive Assessment.
GOAL II:	All students will meet or exceed state math standards as measured by ISAT.

Junior High Level

GOAL I:	All students will read at or above grade level by seventh grade as measured by ThinkLink Learning Predictive Assessment.
GOAL II:	All students will be prepared for high school English and ninth grade Algebra I placement by eighth grade as measured by ThinkLink Leaning Predictive Assessment.
GOAL III:	All students will meet or exceed state math standards as measured by ISAT.

100% of District 86 students will graduate from high school as measured by school district surveys to receiving high schools.

80% of District 86 students will graduate from postsecondary schools as measured by surveys sent to former students.

Building A No Excuses

LEARNING ENVIRONMENT

Joliet Public Schools District 86

What is a "No Excuses" Learning Environment?

A place that refuses to make poverty an excuse for academic failure.

A place where principals are skilled in finding training, and bringing out the best in teachers.

A place that ensures that all children master key subjects, especially reading, math, and fluency in the English language.

A place that bas a safe, orderly and happy environment.

A place where students, of all races and income levels are held to high standards and expectations.

A place that tests constantly to determine whether each and every child is learning.

A place where parents actively support the educational process.

A place that ensures that all children succeed.

A place where teachers are held to the same high standards they hold for students

A place that recognizes that children may learn at different paces.

Superintendent's Vision

I want people who walk into every building in the District to receive the clear message that we are serious about the business of academics. This opinion should be formed because they see:

- Students moving quietly through the halls.
- Teachers/students and students/students interacting respectfully and positively with each other.
- Students completing work assignments and remaining on task.
- Students articulating their goals and reason for being in school.

Superintendent's Standards

1. Every building will have a safe and orderly environment.

    A. There are posted guides for behavioral expectations.
    B. Students are taught the behaviors staff wishes them to display.
    C. Everyone in the school assumes responsibility for student behavior.

2. There is an articulated, consistent approach to discipline.

    A. Principles of Discipline with Dignity are practiced.
    B. Focus is on changing behavior to a self-monitoring, internalized approach.

3. Quality instruction occurs in every classroom.

    A. Professional development and literature review occurs to improve skills.
    B. Instructional planning occurs.
    C. Continuous feedback is given to students regarding effort and improvement actions.
    D. Everyone is on task.
    E. Teachers are teaching and students are learning.
    F. Multiple strategies are utilized - engaged learning, differentiated instruction.

4. High expectations are held by everyone.

    A. Belief in students' ability to learn (effort versus ability thinking).
    B. Student success is highest priority.

5. **Professional climate is created.**

   A. Colleagues help and support each other.
   B. Learning dialogue occurs - what can I do to get better? What new knowledge can be shared?
   C. Staff knows District mission, goals, priorities, focus, expectations and incorporates them into their work.
   D. Accepts responsibility for representing school and District in all that is done.

Each Building will ensure:

1. Safety for Students
2. Learning for Students
3. Respectful Interactions
4. Continuous Feedback
5. Posted Behavioral Expectations
6. Teachers will:

   a) Know District's Mission
   b) Know District's Goals
   c) Participate in staff development activities
   d) Read professional literature
   e) Create a professional environment - dialogue, *dress

* Maintain a professional appearance consistent with expectations for students

Employee Commitment

Interpersonal Relationships

We will be respectful, caring, supportive and helpful of each other. We will adhere to the District rules for student interactions:

a) **No arguing with students**
b) **No yelling at students**
c) **No use of sarcasm with students**

> (Sarcasm is the cruel act of humiliating someone in front of their peers under the guise of humor.)
>
> - Todd Whitaker

Performance

We will put forth our best effort to produce the highest quality product - well educated students. We will perform the duties, tasks and responsibilities for which we are paid.

Proficiency Requirements

We will continue to improve our skills and acquire new knowledge about our work.

District Filter

We will serve as ambassadors for the district by speaking positively about the place where we work. Any criticisms, or negative comments will be developed into specific actions and contributions you can make to help us be all that you would wish.

PARTNERS IN LEARNING

Student-Parent-Teacher-Administrator Agreement

We know that students learn best at ______________________________ School when everyone works together to encourage learning and practice appropriate behavior. This agreement is a promise to work together as a team to help ______________________________ achieve in school. Together, we can improve teaching and learning.

As a student, I pledge to

- ☐ work as hard as I can on mv school assignments.
- ☐ discuss with my parents what I am learning in school.
- ☐ respect myself, my family members, and school staff members.
- ☐ practice the goals or the District Behavior Standard at all times.
- ☐ ask my teacher questions when I don't understand something.
- ☐ use my public or school library frequently
- ☐ limit my TV watching and make time for reading.
- ☐ follow bus safety rules.

Student signature____________________________

As a parent, I pledge to

- ☐ encourage good study habits, including quiet study time at home.
- ☐ talk with my child every day about his or her school activities.
- ☐ reinforce respect for self and others.
- ☐ support the District Behavior Standards and review bus safety roles with my child.
- ☐ beware or my child's progress in school by attending conferences, reviewing school work and calling the teacher or school with questions.

- volunteer for my child's school or district.
- encourage good reading habits by reading to or with my child and by reading myself.
- limit my child's TV viewing and help select worthwhile programs.
- participate in at least 3 parent sessions during the school year.

Parent signature ____________________________

As a teacher, I pledge to

- provide motivating and interesting learning experiences in my classroom.
- explain my instructional goals and grading system to students and parents.
- explain academic and classroom expectations to students and parents.
- provide for two-way communication with parents about what children are learning in school and how families can enhance children's learning at home and in the community.
- respect the uniqueness of my students and their families.
- teach and reinforce the District Behavior Standards, bus safety rules, and class expectations at all times.
- explore what techniques and materials help each child learn best.
- guide students and parents in choosing reading materials and TV programs

Teacher signature____

As a principal/school administrator, I pledge to

- make sure students and parents feel welcome in school.

- ☐ communicate the school's mission and goals to students and parents.
- ☐ offer a variety of ways for families to be partners in their children's learning and to support this school.
- ☐ ensure a safe and nurturing learning environment.
- ☐ implement and promote the District Behavior Standards, bus safety rules, and school expectations at, all times.
- ☐ strengthen the partnership among students, parents, and teachers.
- ☐ act as the instructional leader by supporting teachers in their classrooms.
- ☐ provide opportunities for learning and development to teachers, families, and community members,

Principal signature ____________________________

Mostly importantly, we promise to help each other carry out this agreement.

Signed on this_______________ day of__________________, 2007.

Compañeros en el Aprendizaje

Contrato de Estudiantes-Padres- Maestros(as)-Administradores

Nosotros sabemos que los estudiantes aprenden mejor en la Escuela cuando todos trabajamos juntas con entusiasmo para aprender y practicar la conducta apropiada. Este contrato es una promesa de trabajar unidos como un equipo para ayudar a a triunfar en la escuela. Juntos podemos mejorar la enseñanza y el aprendizaje.

Como estudiante, Yo prometo

- trabajar con gran entusiasmo en mis tareas escolares.
- hablar con mis padres de lo que estoy aprendiendo en la escuela.
- respetarme a mí mismo/a respetar a mi familia, y a miembros de la facultad escolar.
- practicar las metas de las Normas de Comportamiento del Distrito todo el tiempo.
- preguntar a mi maestro/a cuando yo no entiendo algo.
- usar la biblioteca pública o de la escuela con frecuencia.
- limitar mi tiempo para ver televisión y tomar más tiempo para leer
- seguir las reglas de seguridad del autobús.

Firma del estudiante________________________

Como padre, Yo prometo

- apoyar los buenos hábitos para estudiar, incluyendo tiempo para estudiar en casa.
- hablar con mi hijo/a diario de sus actividades escolares.
- reafirmar el respeto por sí mismo/a y por los demás.
- apoyar las Normas de Comportamiento del Distrito y las reglas de seguridad del autobús con mi hijo/a.

- estar al pendiente del progreso de mi hijo/a en la escuela, asistiendo a conferencias, revisando el trabajo de la escuela, y llamando a los maestros/as o a la escuela si tengo preguntas.
- ofrecerme como voluntario/a en la escuela de mi hijo/a o distrito.
- adoptar buenos hábitos de lectura y leer con mi hijo/a.
- limitar el tiempo que mi hijo/a ve televisión y ayudarlo a seleccionar buenos programas.
- participar en tres juntas de padres durante el año escolar.

Firma del padre____

Como Maestro(a), Yo prometo

- proporcionar experiencias interesantes de aprendizaje que motiven a los estudiantes en mi salón de clases.
- explicar mis metas de instrucci6n y el sistema de calificaciones a los estudiantes y a los padres.
- explicar a los estudiantes y padres lo que se espera académicamente y las reglas del sal6n de clases.
- proporcionar un medio de comunicaci6n recíproca con los padres acerca de lo que sus niños/as están aprendiendo en la escuela, y de qué manera las familias los pueden ayudar a aprender más en casa y en la comunidad.
- respetar la individualidad de mis estudiantes y sus familias.
- enseñar y reafirmar las Normas de Comportamiento del Distrito, las reglas de seguridad del autobús, y las metas de la clase todo el tiempo
- explorar el modo y los materiales que puedan ayudar para que cada niño/a aprenda mejor.
- guiar a los estudiantes y a sus padres a seleccionar materiales de lectura y programas de televisión

Firma del Maestro/a ____

Como Director/Administrador de la Escuela, Yo prometo

- ☐ asegurarme de que los estudiantes y sus padres se sientan bienvenidos en la escuela.
- ☐ comunicar la misi6n y las metas de la escuela a los estudiantes y a sus padres.
- ☐ ofrecer varias maneras para que las familias puedan ser participantes dcl aprendizaje de sus hijos/as y apoyen a la escuela.
- ☐ ofrecer un ambiente de aprendizaje seguro y educativo.
- ☐ implementar y promover las Normas de Comportamiento del Distrito, las reglas dc seguridad del autobús, y las metas de la escuela todo el tiempo.
- ☐ reforzar el compañerismo entre estudiantes, padres y maestros/as.
- ☐ actuar como el líder instruccional apoyando a los/as maestros/as en sus salones de clase.
- ☐ proporcionar oportunidades de aprendizaje y desarrollo para los maestros/as, las familias y los miembros de la comunidad.

Firma del Director/a____________________________________

Y sobre todo, muy importante, nosotros prometemos ayudarnos los unos a los otros para cumplir este contrato.

Firmado el _______día de_______, 2007

Self-Reflection Questions

1. Are you the "right" person on the "right" bus?
2. Do you support the work of others or are you a "naysayer"?
3. Are you self-motivated?
4. Are you self-disciplined?
5. Are you making a contribution?
6. Are you doing the job for which you are paid?
7. Is your work a mission, and not just a job?
8. Are you finding ways to continuously improve the way you do your work?
9. Do you conduct yourself as a professional? (Professional is a way of acting and looking, not just how many degrees you have.)
10. Do you own the children we serve?
11. Do you show respect to all in your environment?
12. Have you planned how your work will occur?
13. Do you have a self-improvement plan?
14. Have you faced the brutal truth about your work and then moved forward to make things better?
15. Do you have the desire to be great at what you do?
16. Do you follow the plan in place or are you doing your own thing?
17. Are you part of the school team? The District team?
18. Are you on the same path as everyone else or have you gone down a different path?

Reference List for Elementary School 2007-2008

1. Active Literacy Across The Curriculum by Jacobs
2. Building Background Knowledge for Academic Success by Marzano
3. Classroom Instruction that Works with English Language Learners by Jane Hill and Kathleen Flynn
4. Creating an Inclusive School 2nd Edition by Villa. Thousand
5. Data Driven Differentiation in the Standards-Based Classroom by Gregory, Kuzmich
6. Dealing With Difficult Parents And With Parents in Difficult Situations by Whitaker, Fiore
7. Differentiating Instruction for Students With Learning Disabilities by Bender
8. Differentiated Instructional Strategies for Reading in the Content Areas by Chapman, King
9. Dual Language Essentials by Freeman. Freeman, and Mercuri
10. 55 Essentials by Ron Clark
11. Hear Our Cry, Boys in Crisis by Paul Slocumb
12. Ready lo Use Social Skills Lessons & Activities for Grades PrcK-K by Weltmann Begun
13. Ready to Use Social Skills Lessons & Activities for Grades l-3 by Weltmann Begun
14. Ready to Use Social Skills Lessons & Activities for Grades 4-6 by Weltmann Begun
15. Removing The Mask: Giftedness in Poverty by Slocumb, Payne
16. Results Now by Schmoker
17. Seven Simple Secrets by Breaux and Whitaker
18. Teach Me I Dare You by Brough, Bergman, Holt
19. The At Risk Student In Our Schools by McCarney, Wunderlich, Bauer
20. The Teacher's Resource Guide by McCarney, Wunderlich, Bauer
21. Through Ebony Eyes by Gail Thompson
22. Whatever It Takes by DuFour, DuFour, Eaker, Karhanek
23. What Great Teachers Do Differently by Whitaker

Reference List for Junior High School 2007-2008

1. Creating an Inclusive School 2nd Edition by Villa, Thousand
2. Building Reading Comprehension Habits in Grades 6-8 by Zwiers
3. Building Background Knowledge for Academic Success by Marzano
4. Classroom Instruction that Works with English Language Learners by Jane Hill and Kathleen Flynn
5. Dealing With Difficult Parents And With Parents in Difficult Situations by Whitaker, Fiore
6. Developing Academic Tlunla.ng Skills in Grades 6-12 by Zwicrs
7. Differentiated Instruction for Middle and High School Teacher by Benjamin
8. Differentiating Instruction for Students With Learning Disabilities by Bender
9. Dual Language Essentials by Freeman, Freeman, and Mercuri
10. 55 Essentials by Ron Clark
11. Hear Our Cry, Boys in Crisis by Paul Slocumb
12. Practical Approaches for Teaching Reading and Writing in Middle Schools by Morretta and Ambrossini
13. Ready to Use Social Skills Lessons & Activities for Grades 4-6 by Weltmann Begun
14. Ready to Use Social Skills Lessons & Activities for Grades 7-12 by Weltmann Begun
15. Removing The Mask: Giftedness in Poverty by Slocumb, Payne
16. Results Now by Schmoker
17. Seven Simple Secrets by Breaux and Whitaker
18. Struggling Adolescent Readers by Moore, Alvermann, Hinchman
19. Teach Me I Dare You by Brough, Bergman, Holl
20. The Al Risk Student In Our Schools by McCarney, Wunderlich, Bauer
21. The Teacher's Resource Guide by McCarne,y, Wunderlich, Bauer
22. Through Ebony Eyes by Gail Thompson
23. Whatever It Takes by Dufour, Dufour, Eaker, Karhanek
24. What Great Teachers Do Differently by Whitaker

Good Reads

Interested in knowing what the country's top superintendents are reading? Here's a look at the books recommended by AASA's 2005 state superintendents of the year:

- Blink: The Power of Thinking Without Thinking. by Malcolm Gladwell
- Collapse: How Societies Choose to Fail or Succeed, by Jared Diamond
- The Contrarian's Guide to Leadership, by Steven B. Sample
- Emotional Intelligence: Why it Can Matter More Than IQ, by Daniel Goleman
- The Four Agreements: A Practical Guide to Personal Freedom (A Toltec Wisdom Book). by Don Miguel Ruiz
- Good to Great: Why Some Companies Make the Leap... And Others Don't, by Jim Collins
- How the Brain Learns, by David A. Sousa
- The Shame of a Nation: The Restoration of Apartheid Schooling in America, by Jonathan Kozol
- The Superintendent's Field book: A Guide for Leaders of Learning, by Nelda Cambron-McCabe et al.
- Thinking for a Change: 11 Ways Highly Successful People Approach Life and Work, by John C. Maxwell
- The Tipping Point: How Little Things Can Make a Big Difference, by Malcolm Gladwell
- The World Is Flat: A Brief History of the Twenty-First Century, by Thomas L. Friedman

Recommended Reading From ASCD...

- The Art of School Leadership (2005) by Thomas R. Hoerr
- Assessing Student Outcomes: Performance Assessment Using the Dimensions of Learning Model (1993) by Robert J. Marzano. Debra Pickering and Jay McTighe
- Assessment in the Learning Organization: Shifting the Paradigm (1995) edited by Arthur L. Costa and Bena Kallick
- Classroom Management That Works: Research-Based Strategies for Every Teacher (2003) by Robert J. Marzano, Jana S. Marzano and Debra J. Pickering
- Connecting Character to Conduct Helping Students Do the Right Things (2000) by Rita Stein, Roberta Richin, Richard Banyon, Francine Banyon and Marc Stein
- Meeting Standards Through Integrated Curriculum (2004) by Susan M. Drake and Rebecca C. Burns
- The New Principal's Fieldbook: Strategies for Success (2004) by Pam Robbins and Harvey Alvy
- The Result's Fieldbook: Practical Strategies from Dramatically Improved Schools (2001) by Michael J. Schmoker
- Staying Centered: Curriculum Leadership in A Turbulent Era (1998) by Steven J. Gross

Community Engagement Examples

Children for Peace-The capstone of our school year was the theater performance for the Children for Peace initiative. Parents, friends, family members attended to see the talents of our students. This brought the community together for something positive.

Other actions:

District Newsletter-a districtwide newsletter was sent to all parents and community organizations allowing the district to tell our story about the positive actions occurring in the district (A perfect counter to some of the negative news the local newspaper often focused on).

Foundation Event-An annual baseball game that brought in former known baseball players to join with us. This event served as a fundraiser for the foundation. We were also able to utilize the relatively new city baseball field.

Board meetings- Many of our board meetings were held on school sites which provided principals the opportunity to present information to board members about their schools and to recognize staff and students. Parents would also be in attendance to see their schools highlighted.

Children For Peace Project

September 2002

Developed by:
Dr. Phyllis M. Wilson
Mrs. Carol Sossong
Mrs. Sandra Zalewski
Ms. Anna White

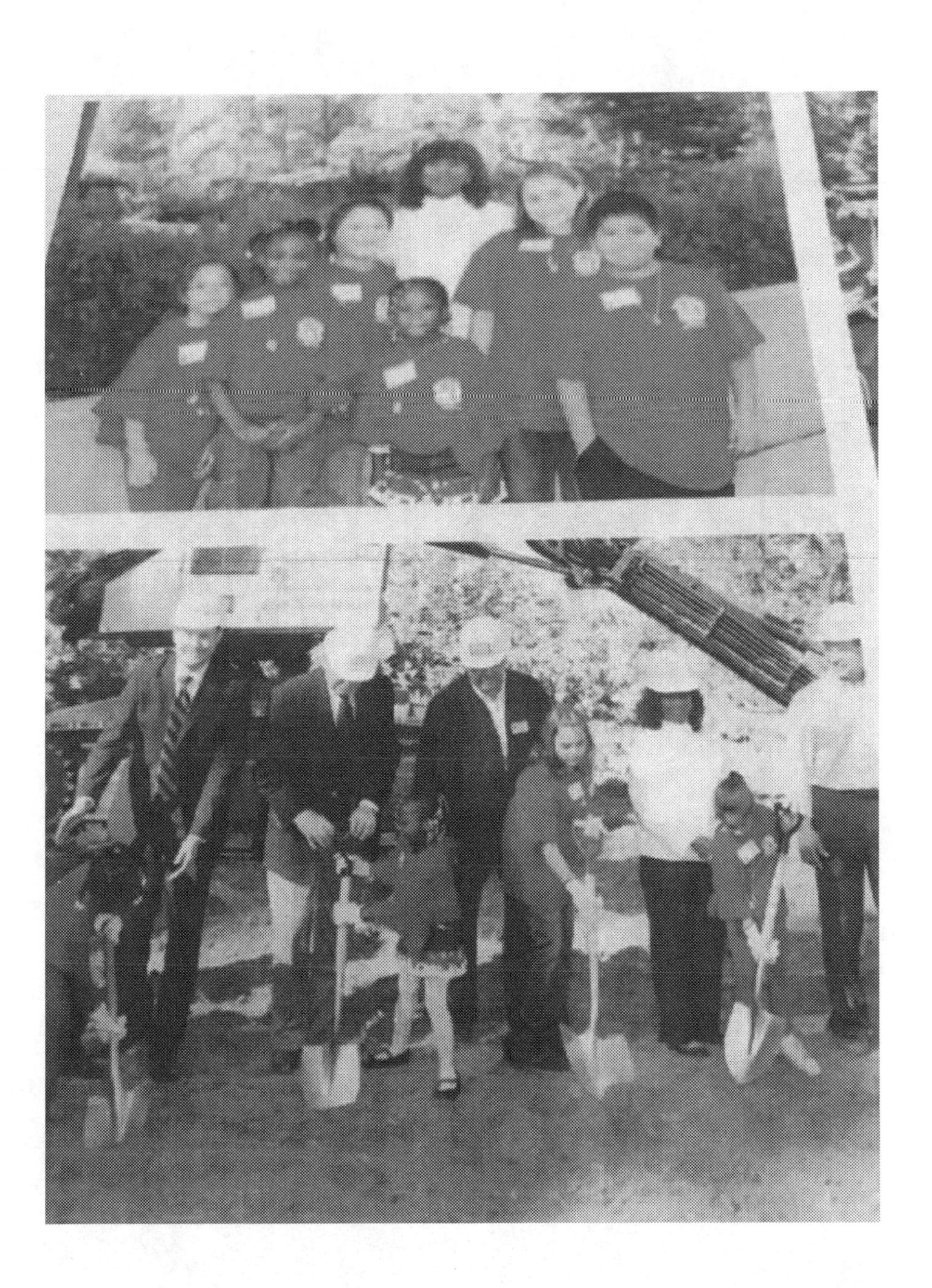

JOLIET GRADE SCHOOLS

FOUNDATION

AWARDS CLASSROOM GRANTS

'he Joliet Grade Schools Foundation for ucational Excellence approved grants to rict 86 teachers and staff totaling nearly 000 to enhance educational opportunities ır students at our schools.

are excited that we can make a positive t to the students in District 86 through rants," said Glen Marcum, president oliet Grade Schools Foundation. "The vill assist teachers and staff with s that are not funded by the school

ion, thank you to everyone that the Foundation's eighth annual seball Fundraiser at the end of

September at Silver Cross Field. Former Major League Baseball players Steve Garvey, Jay Johnstone, Bill Lee, Chuck McElroy, Jerry Reuss, and Steve Trout spent a day playing baseball with local businessmen to raise mon for our foundation. Sponsors of the event included ExxonMobil, Robert W. Baird & Co. Chevron Energy Solutions, First Midwest Ba and Healy, Bender, and Associates.

In the past seven years, the Joliet Grade Schools Foundation has awarded 168 class grants totaling more than $238,000 to Dist 86 employees. To learn more about the Found call Sandy Zalewski at (815) 740-3196 ext

lations to the following schools who h
rants for the 2010-2011 school year:

oks	$1,197.20	
Fiction		
books	$1,484.00	
	$381.45	
ers	$1,500.00	
	$1,850.00	
	$1,253.34	

Marycrest Early Childhood Cente

- Materials for student prop boxes
- Sling Swing
- Handwriting workshop and materials
- Music CDs, books, instruments, and CD/Cassette Player

Parks Cultural Studies Acade

- Time for Kids Weekly news magazines
- Student sensory intervention materials

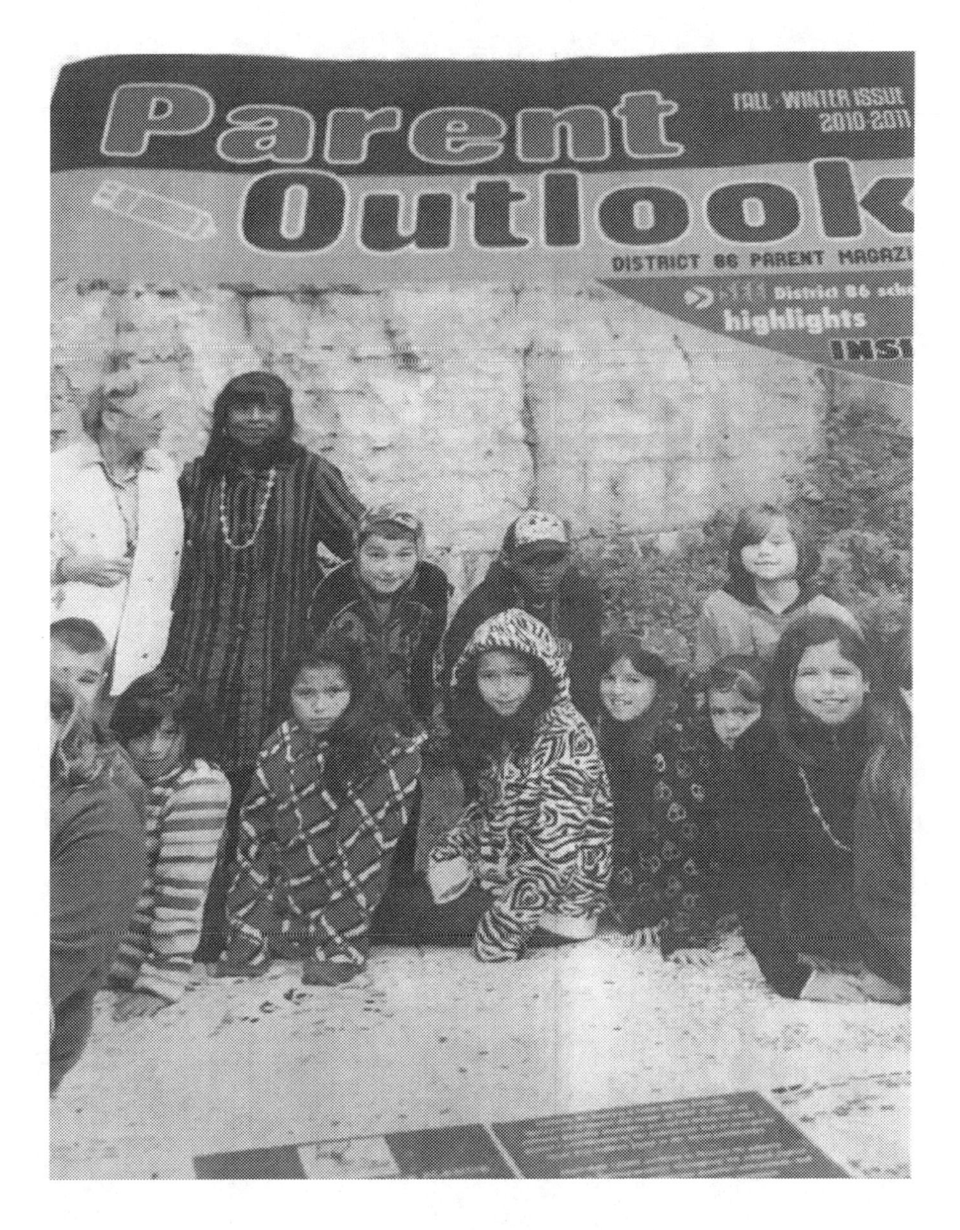
Parent
Outlook
FALL · WINTER ISSUE
2010·2011
DISTRICT 86 PARENT
highlights

Joliet Grade School District 86 SCHOOL NEWS

Culbertson students (from left to right) Nicholas Hass, Kailyn Stovall, and Kenneth Edwards enjoy their ice cream reward.

DISTRICT 86 ASSISTS HAITI EARTHQUAKE VICTIMS

Thank you to Joliet Grade School District 86 students, families, and staff that donated money for the victims of the Haiti earthquake. The Children for Peace "Helping Hands for Haiti" fundraiser raised over $8,200 for the American Red Cross.

A.O. Marshall and T.E. Culbertson Elementary Schools received ice cream parties for their outstanding efforts.

Donations:

T.E. Culbertson Elementary
1,034.54

M.J. Cunningham Elementary 550.57

Dirksen Junior High
172.31

Eisenhower Academy
426.24

Farragut Elementary
[illegible]

A.O. Marshall Elementary
1,306.34

Marycrest Early Childhood Center
765.10

Parks Cultural Studies Academy
489.95

Pershing Elementary
388.82

JOLIET SUPERINTENDI BY LEWIS UNI

Lewis University presented the De La Salle Award to seven members of the community during a special ceremony on April 11, 2010. The De La Salle Award is presented each year to individuals who provide extraordinary service and leadership for the benefit of the community and region.

"I am honored and privileged to be a 2010 recipient of the John De La Salle Award," said Dr. Wilson. "My recognition represents the many people who have supported me throughout my tenure with District 86."

Dr. Wilson is Superintendent for Joliet Public Schools District 86, overseeing 11,144 preschool through junior high students and over 1,400 employees in 23 buildings.

(From left to right) Joliet Grade
Wilson is presented with a De
In the Community by Lewis Un
FSC.

GOMPERS JUNIOR HIGH WI

Joliet Grade Schools

News for the District 86 Community

Message from Superintendent

Dear Community Member:

On behalf of the Board of School Inspectors and District 86, we extend our heartfelt thanks to the Joliet community for the tremendous support our schools have received over the years. At this time of uncertain financial times in Illinois, we need your support more than ever.

We have a firm commitment to financial stability and responsible management of taxpayer's money. In addition, we will continue to extend our 1999 Education Fund referendum dollars as far into the future as possible.

As we move into a period of economic uncertainty, we will strive to maintain our current class sizes of 26 students and try not to cut programs that directly affect our students and families.

Sincerely,

Phyllis M. Wilson, Ph.D.
Superintendent

istrict 86 Schools Make Illinois Honor Roll

he Illinois State Board of
ation (ISBE) and Northern
s University announced that
hools, including six Joliet
Schools, made the 2009
Honor Roll for their continued
ic progress. All of these
ling schools are being
for their accomplishments
g progress toward or
ng academic excellence.
ower Academy received
ic Excellence Award for
ar in a row. Dirksen
, Forest Park I.E.,
ferson Elementary,
mentary, and Taft
schools were named
ools. Thomas
mentary also won an
rovement Award.
proud of our schools
t," said District 86
Dr. Phyllis Wilson.
of students have
hard and I am glad
to see that their efforts are being recognized."

"These Honor Roll schools include struggling schools that have undertaken large reform efforts as well as high-performing schools that have maintained excellence even as the bar to making Adequate Yearly Progress grows higher," said State Superintendent Christopher A. Koch. "This kind of achievement requires nothing less than sheer hard work and dedication on the part of administrators, teachers, parents and students."

Northern Illinois University worked with ISBE to establish criteria, identify winners of the awards, and administer the Illinois Honor Roll, which is divided into three categories: Spotlight Schools; Academic Excellence; and Academic Improvement. Each award has unique criteria that best reflect the diverse circumstances of Illinois schools.

Spotlight Schools
Recognizes 425 high-poverty, high-performing schools that are beating the odds to overcoming the achievement gap.

Academic Excellence Awards
438 schools have sustained high performance over at least three ye

Academic Improvement Awar
147 schools are showing substan
gains over three years.

The 2009 honor roll roster inc
elementary, middle and high sch
including charter schools, and
represents 362 school districts s
wide. The 975 schools earned a
1,110 awards in the three categ

Author Comments

*Please note that in order to ensure compliance with the copyright laws, much of the content in the presentations that I provided for staff has been reduced to the acceptable amount. What is shown are examples of what was shared. The presentations provided to staff utilized specific concepts with references from experts in the field included to reinforce the concepts as well as provide the guidance and strategies that worked best for my student population.

I have been chosen
to save the world

one child at a time

A Take Away For You

As we close the last pages of the book, there is one final assignment I would like you to take with you. It is as follows:

Look carefully at the picture titled "I Have Been Chosen to Save The World One Child At A Time". What thoughts come to mind? What is the message that the picture wishes to send?

How would you share this message with others in a developed program or a presentation?

Who would be your target audience for sharing this message?

Now put all of your thoughts and ideas into a finished product and go forward to share your finished product with others. And, guess what? When you do, you will be changing the world. Good luck to you.

32_OneChildAtATime